W' Lilly Heard

by
Judy
Nayer

illustrated
by
Rick
Stromoski

Scott Foresman

Editorial Offices: Glenview, Illinois • New York, New York
Sales Offices: Reading, Massachusetts • Duluth, Georgia
Glenview, Illinois • Carrollton, Texas • Menlo Park, California

Lilly Pup sat on her bed.
She started to read.

Then she heard something.
It was the baby.
"I can't read here," she said.

Lilly Pup started to read.
Then she heard something.

It was her father.
"I can't read here," she said.

Lilly Pup went out.
She started to read.

Then she heard something.
It was her mother.
"I can't read here!" she said.

Lilly Pup looked around.
"I like my father.
I like my mother.

I even like the baby.
But I like to read too.
It is what I like to do most.
And I can't read here!"

Lilly Pup walked to a quiet spot.
She walked and walked.
She didn't hear a peep.

Lilly started to read.
She read most of her book.
Then she went to sleep.

Lilly Pup heard something.
She heard her mother.
She heard her father.
She even heard the baby.

"There you are!" they said.
"We have been looking all over!"

Lilly Pup went home.
She got in bed.

Lilly Pup liked to read.

But now she didn't want to read.

"You read," she told her mother.

Lilly Pup heard something.
It was something she liked a lot.
She heard her mother reading.
And that was just fine.